PORT MOODY PUBLIC LIBRARY

Pebble™

Desert Animals

Scorpions

by William John Ripple

Consulting Editor: Gail Saunders-Smith, PhD

Consultant: Michael A. Mares, PhD, Former Director,
Sam Noble Oklahoma Museum of Natural History
University of Oklahoma, Norman, Oklahoma

Mankato, Minnesota

Pebble Books are published by Capstone Press,
151 Good Counsel Drive, P.O. Box 669, Mankato, Minnesota 56002.
www.capstonepress.com

Copyright © 2005 by Capstone Press. All rights reserved.
No part of this publication may be reproduced in whole or in part,
or stored in a retrieval system, or transmitted in any form or by any means,
electronic, mechanical, photocopying, recording, or otherwise,
without written permission of the publisher.
For information regarding permission, write to Capstone Press,
151 Good Counsel Drive, P.O. Box 669, Dept. R, Mankato, Minnesota 56002.
Printed in the United States of America

1 2 3 4 5 6 10 09 08 07 06 05

Library of Congress Cataloging-in-Publication Data
Ripple, William John.
Scorpions / by William John Ripple.
p. cm.—(Desert animals)
Includes bibliographical references and index.
ISBN 0-7368-3637-3 (hardcover)
1. Scorpions—Juvenile literature. I. Title. II. Desert animals (Mankato, Minn.)
QL458.7.R57 2005
595.4'6—dc22 2004013301

Summary: Simple text and photographs introduce the habitat, appearance, and behavior of scorpions.

Note to Parents and Teachers

The Desert Animals set supports national science standards related to life science. This book describes and illustrates scorpions. The photographs support early readers in understanding the text. The repetition of words and phrases helps early readers learn new words. This book also introduces early readers to subject-specific vocabulary words, which are defined in the Glossary section. Early readers may need assistance to read some words and to use the Table of Contents, Glossary, Read More, Internet Sites, and Index sections of the book.

Table of Contents

What Are Scorpions?

Scorpions are arachnids.
Scorpions are related
to spiders and ticks.

Scorpions are brown,
black, or yellow.

places where scorpions live

Where Scorpions Live

Scorpions live around the world. Some scorpions live in deserts.

Body Parts

Scorpions have
curved tails
with stingers.

pincers

Scorpions have
sharp pincers.

What Scorpions Do

Female scorpions
carry their young
until the young
are ready to hunt.

Most scorpions hunt
for food at night.
They look for insects,
spiders, and other
small animals to eat.

Scorpions catch prey
with their pincers.
Scorpions sting prey
with their stingers.

Scorpions rest under logs or rocks during the day.

Glossary

arachnid—a small animal that has eight legs and two body sections; scorpions, spiders, and ticks are arachnids.

desert—an area of dry land with few plants; deserts receive very little rain.

hunt—to find and kill animals for food

pincer—a body part that is like a claw; scorpions use their pincers to catch prey.

prey—an animal hunted by another animal for food

stinger—a long, sharp hollow body part; poison flows through the stinger into the prey.

Read More

Berger, Melvin, and Gilda Berger. *Sting!: A Book About Dangerous Animals.* Hello Science Reader! New York: Scholastic, 2003.

Halfmann, Janet. *Scorpions.* Nature's Predators. San Diego: Kidhaven Press, 2003.

Harman, Amanda. *Scorpions.* Nature's Children. Danbury, Conn.: Grolier Educational, 2001.

Internet Sites

FactHound offers a safe, fun way to find Internet sites related to this book. All of the sites on FactHound have been researched by our staff.

Here's how:

1. Visit *www.facthound.com*
2. Type in this special code **0736836373** for age-appropriate sites. Or enter a search word related to this book for a more general search.
3. Click on the **Fetch It** button.

FactHound will fetch the best sites for you!

WWW.FACTHOUND.COM SM

Index

Word Count: 87
Grade: 1
Early-Intervention Level: 12

Editorial Credits
Mari C. Schuh, editor; Patrick D. Dentinger, set designer and illustrator; Steve Meunier, photo researcher; Scott Thoms, photo editor

Photo Credits
Ann & Rob Simpson, 20
Bruce Coleman Inc./Gary Schultz, 8; Jan Taylor, 18; J. C. Carton, 14; John Bell, 12
Corbis/Mark L. Stephenson, 16
Digital Vision, 1, 6
James P. Rowan, cover, 4
Minden Pictures/Claus Meyer, 10